Ready
Text Collection

PEARSON

Glenview, Illinois • Boston, Massachusetts • Chandler, Arizona • Hoboken, New Jersey

PEARSON

ISBN-13: 978-0-328-85798-2
ISBN-10:   0-328-85798-X
4 16

Exploring Communities

Judith Caseley

A Community Adventure

Charlie's class was studying community.
"A community," said the teacher, "is a group of
people who live or work in the same area, or who
have something in common with each other."
She gave each of the children a black, speckled
notebook. "Visit the people and places in your
community. Take your notebooks and explore."

"Homework?" asked Mama when school was over.
"Yes," said Charlie. "What is my community?"
"Let's take a walk and find out," said Mama.
Charlie's teacher left the building and waved
good-bye.
"Teacher!" said Charlie. "Should I write her
name down?"
"Absolutely," said Mama. "Your teacher is
a big part of your community."

6

Charlie wrote *teacher*. Then he
wrote *school* and drew pictures
of some of his other teachers.

Mama and Charlie walked through the park. The garbage collectors were emptying trash cans. A sign on one trash can said, "Keep your park clean."

Charlie picked up a soda bottle and threw it in the trash can that said "Recycle." Then he wrote the word *garbage*, and Mama spelled *collector* for him, and Charlie copied the word *recycle*.

On the way into town, Charlie tripped over something.
It was someone's lost wallet, and Charlie showed it to Mama.
"Maybe we should take it to the police station," he said.

"Good idea," Mama told him, and they walked to the
police station, where they met Joe the police officer
and gave the wallet to him.

"You're a good part of my community," said Charlie.

"So are you," said Joe.

Charlie wrote *police station*. Then he wrote *Joe*
and drew a star next to his name.

"You need a haircut," Mama told Charlie as they left the police station.

"Barber shop!" said Charlie. "So smart," said Mama.

12

Charlie wrote *barber shop*. Then George cut
his hair, and Charlie wrote *George* and drew a
pair of scissors.
"Very handsome," said Mama. "Now I need
to buy stamps."

"Post office!" cried Charlie.

"My genius!" said Mama.

Charlie wrote *post office* while a lady behind
the counter whose name was Evelyn sold Mama
the kind of stamps that didn't need licking. Charlie
wrote *Evelyn* and drew his own special stamp.

15

"Did you ever thank Grandma for the toy
she sent you?" Mama asked.
"We'll buy a card for Grandma at the pharmacy!"
said Charlie, writing *farmacy*.
"It's not a farm," said Mama,
changing the *f* to *ph*.
Then they picked out
a thank-you card, and
Charlie waved to the
man who was behind
the pharmacy counter.
Charlie wrote his name
and spelled *pharmacy*
correctly.

16

"I'm running out of money,"
Mama said to Charlie.
"Bank!" said Charlie.
"Bingo!" said Mama.
Charlie read the badge on the
bank teller's blouse.
Her name was Ms. Chung,
and she gave Mama money
while Charlie wrote her name
with a long line of dollar signs.

17

"All this hard work is making me hungry,"
said Charlie.

"Really?" said Mama. "And where shall we go?"

"To Henry's Luncheonette!" Charlie told her.

"Write it down," said Mama.

Then Charlie had chocolate milk, and Mama had coffee,
and Charlie drew a picture of Juanita, the waitress.
Mama pulled a book out of her pocketbook.

"Have you finished reading this?"
she asked Charlie.

18

"Yes! Library!" Charlie shouted.

"You're a whiz!" said Mama.

They walked down the street past the fire station.
Uncle Kerry was polishing the fire engine.
Charlie wrote *fire station*. He drew a fire and
a hose and wrote *Uncle Kerry*, with five hearts
and five stars for his favorite uncle.
Uncle Kerry put a fire hat on Charlie's
head and carried him around
on his shoulders.

They left the firehouse and went
to the library, where they checked out some books.
Charlie wrote the librarian's name and drew a picture of her.

"It's time to meet Papa at
the train," said Mama.
"Train station!" said Charlie.
"What a brain!" said Mama.

Papa stepped off the train and waved good-bye to the conductor.
Charlie hugged Papa. Mama kissed Papa. Charlie showed Papa his "Community" book. Then he wrote *train station* and *train conductor*, and they headed down Main Street.

23

24

"Some flowers would be nice," said Mama sweetly.

"Flower shop!" said Charlie.

"Isn't he smart?" said Mama.

Papa agreed, and Charlie drew a picture in his notebook of the florist holding a bouquet of flowers in her hands. Papa bought Mama a bunch of red tulips and said, "Is anyone hungry?"

"Pizza parlor!" said Charlie.
"Sounds good," said Papa.
"Write it down while
we order," Mama
told him.

Louis
brought them
a pizza—half
pepperoni and half
mushroom—and they ate it all.
Charlie wrote *Louis* next to *pizza
parlor*, and they headed for home.

Charlie played trucks with Papa.
He read books with Mama.
Then it was time for bed.

"Mama! Papa!" Charlie called from his room.

"What?" said Mama.

"What?" said Papa.

"I forgot," said Charlie.

"You forgot what?" said Papa.

"Community," said Charlie.

"It's all down in your notebook," Mama told him.

"Not the very best part. The best part of all!"

"Tell us," said Mama.

"We're listening," said Papa.

"Home!" said Charlie.

"I forgot about home!"

"Write it down in the morning,"
Mama whispered to Charlie.

"Now go to sleep."

"Sleep tight," said Papa.

"Kiss, kiss," said Mama.

"Good night," said Charlie.

In the morning Charlie ate breakfast. He took out his notebook and sat on the porch. The mailman walked by, carrying a package. The plumber pulled up across the street. The gardener began mowing the neighbor's lawn. Charlie drew a picture and wrote the word *home*. Then he wrote *My Community* across the front of the book. His day had begun.

Places
in My Neighborhood

by Shelly Lyons

What Is a Neighborhood?

A neighborhood is a community filled with different places to see. Each place has a special purpose that meets our needs.

WHOLESALE & RETAIL

35

Places to Live

Mia's home is in the city.
Her apartment is in a building
with many other apartments.

Jack lives in a house
in a small town.
His street is lined with homes.

Places to Keep Us Safe

Carlos visits the fire station in his neighborhood. The firefighters rush to put out a fire.

Devon visits the police station.
The officer tells him
not to talk to strangers.

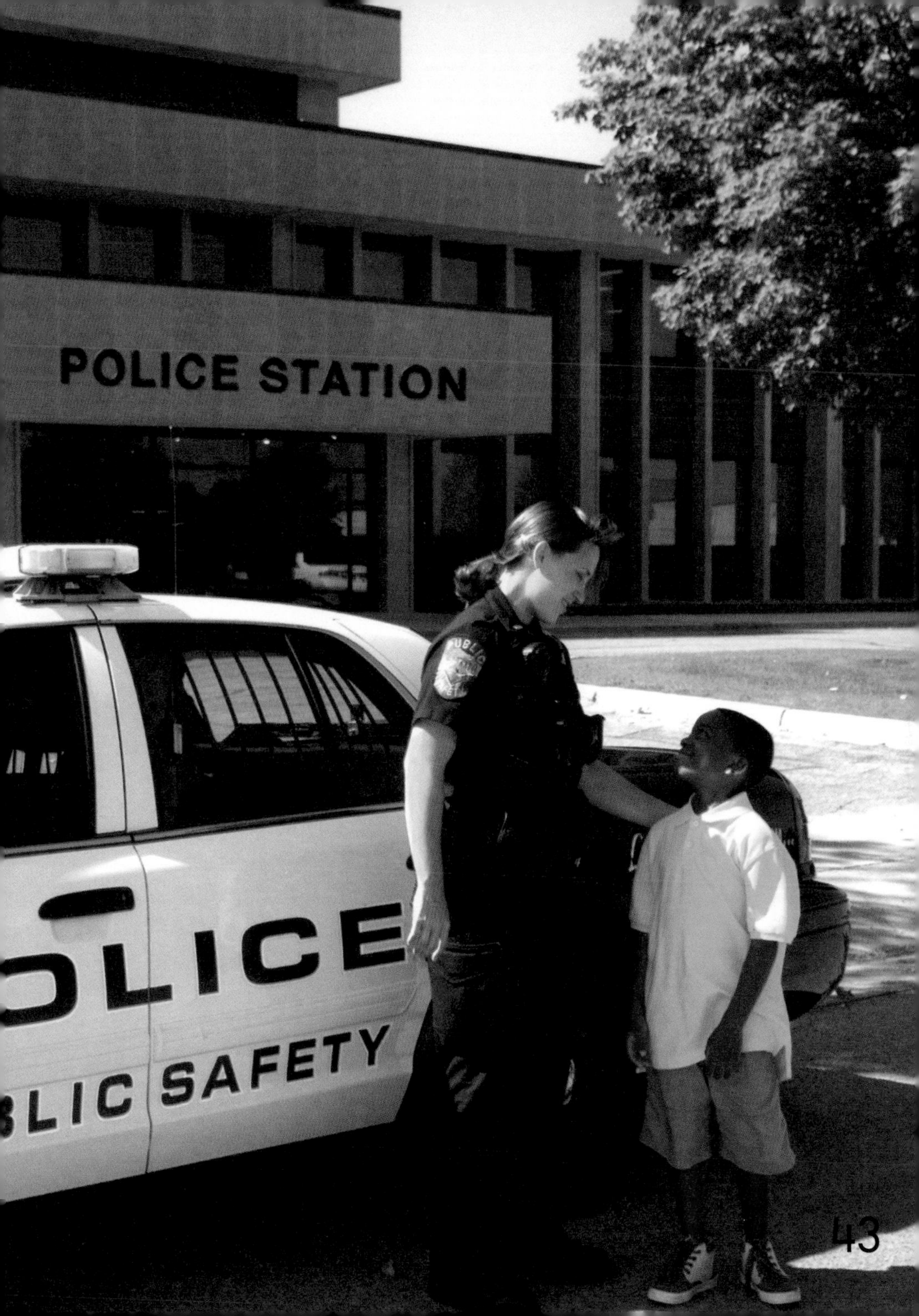
POLICE STATION
POLICE
BLIC SAFETY

At the clinic,

a nurse gives Lila a shot.

She feels better when

she gets a bandage.

45

Places to Find Things

Justin bikes to the library
in his neighborhood.
He checks out books
about dinosaurs.

Jen wants fruit and milk.

At the grocery store

her dad finds fresh grapefruit.

Neighborhoods can be big or small.
What places do you see in your neighborhood?

Glossary

apartment—a home that has its own rooms and front door, but which shares outside walls and a roof with other apartments

bandage—a covering that protects cuts and wounds

community—a group of people who live in the same area

grocery store—a store that sells food items

station—a place or building where a certain service is based

This Is My Community

by Carlos Elliot

Sung to the tune of "Twinkle, Twinkle, Little Star"

This is where I live and play,
Work and shop most every day.

Here's my home and here's my street.
This is where my neighbors meet.

Lots of people live near me.
This is my community!

53

Our Block

by Lois Lenski

Our block is a nice one,
The best in town;
On each side row houses
With steps coming down.

Our block is noisy,
We yell and shout—
Women at the windows,
Children running out.

Our block has music—
Even a band!
We give a block party,
It sure is grand!

We hang up flags
And bunting too;
We dance to the music
All night through.

We dance till morning,
And then we rest;
Our block is a nice one—
The very best.

55

SING A SONG OF CITIES

by Lee Bennett Hopkins

Sing a song of cities.
If you do,
Cities will sing back
  to you.

They'll sing in subway roars and rumbles,
People-laughs, machine-loud grumbles.

Sing a song of cities.
If you do,
Cities will sing back.

Cities will sing back
  to you.

Skyscraper

by Dennis Lee

Skyscraper, skyscraper,
Scrape me some sky:
Tickle the sun
While the stars go by.

Tickle the stars
While the sun's climbing high,
Then skyscraper, skyscraper
Scrape me some sky.

Manhattan Lullaby

by Norma Farber

Lulled by rumble, babble, beep,
let these little children sleep;
let these city girls and boys
dream a music in the noise,
hear a tune their city plucks
up from buses, up from trucks
up from engines wailing *fire!*
up ten stories high, and higher,
up from hammers, rivets, drills,
up tall buildings, over sills,
up where city children sleep,
lulled by rumble, babble, beep.

UNIT 6 • ACKNOWLEDGMENTS

Text

On the Town: A Community Adventure, by Judith Caseley. Published by HarperCollins Publishers.

Excerpted from *Places in My Neighborhood,* by Shelly Lyons. Copyright © 2003 by Capstone. All rights reserved.

"This Is My Community," from *Scott Foresman Social Studies: All Together* by Carlos Elliot. Copyright © 2003 by Pearson Education, Inc., or its affiliates. Used by permission. All rights reserved.

"Our Block," by Lois Lenski. Copyright © by Lois Lenski. Reprinted by permission of SLL/Sterling Lord Literistic, Inc.

"Sing a Song of Cities," from *City I Love* by Lee Bennett Hopkins, illustrated by Marcellus Hall. Text copyright © 1995 by Lee Bennett Hopkins. First appeared in *Good Rhymes, Good Times,* published by HarperCollins Publishers. Reprinted by permission of Curtis Brown, Ltd. Illustrations copyright © 2009 by Marcellus Hall. Used by permission of Abrams Books for Young Readers, an imprint of Harry N. Abrams, Inc., New York. All rights reserved.

"Skyscraper," from *Alligator Pie* by Dennis Lee. *Alligator Pie* published in 1974 by Macmillan of Canada and in 2012 by HarperCollins Canada. Copyright © 1974 by Dennis Lee. Used with permission of the author.

"Manhattan Lullaby," by Norma Farber. Copyright © by Thomas Farber, 1827 Virginia St, Berkeley, CA 94703.

Illustrations

53 Apryl Stott, **54–55** Paula Becker, **58–59** Levente Szabó

Photographs

33 Tom Fawls/Dreamstime; **47** Phi2/Getty Images